WACKY COMPARISONS
HOW HEAVY?

Wacky Ways to Compare Weight

BY MARK WEAKLAND   iLLUSTRATED BY BiLL BOLTON

How heavy is a **bus**?

How heavy is a **dog**?

Are they as heavy as a **MOUSE** or a **frog**?

Look inside, and you will see

just how heavy things can be!

PICTURE WINDOW BOOKS
a capstone imprint

1 bulldog with a stubby tail

weighs the same as

167 hamburgers on a scale.

How heavy is **1** yellow bus?

It equals **4** hippos, each making a fuss.

1 bus = 12 tons (11 metric tons); 1 hippo = 2.8 tn. (2.5 t)

5

How much does a **triceratops** weigh?

The same as
4.2 million
gummy bears, I dare say.

1 triceratops = 10.5 tn. (9.5 t): 1 gummy bear = 0.08 oz. (2.3 g)

How many MARSHMALLOWS will a hedgehog munch to equal its weight? **120.** That's a bunch!

8

1 hedgehog = 30 oz. (850 g); 1 marshmallow = 0.25 oz. (7.1 g)

The weight of **1** panda bear munching bamboo

equals **709** billiard balls,

colorful and new.

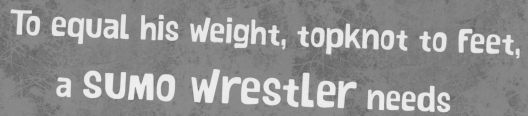

To equal his weight, topknot to feet,
a **SUMO wrestler** needs

1,424 treats.

1 toilet, shiny and white, weighs nearly as much as

98 bullfrogs jumping out of sight.

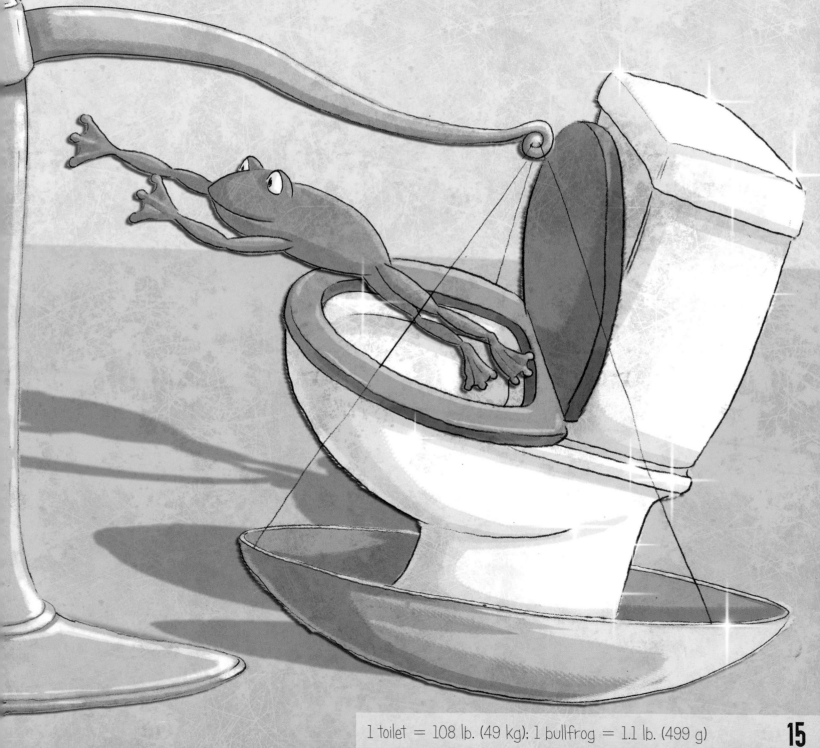

1 toilet = 108 lb. (49 kg); 1 bullfrog = 1.1 lb. (499 g)

How many milk cartons equal **1** cow?

2,222

1 cow = 1,200 lb. (544 kg); 1 carton = 0.54 lb. (245 g)

1 glowing pumpkin in need of braces

weighs the same as

7 guinea pigs making faces.

1 pumpkin = 15 lb. (6.8 kg); 1 guinea pig = 33.5 oz. (950 g)

19

How much does a **bulldozer** weigh?

The same as **19,000 kittens** ready to play.

1 bulldozer = 19 tn. (17.2 t); 1 kitten = 2 lb. (907 g)

3.2 million mice, whisker to tail,
weigh the same as **1** big blue whale.

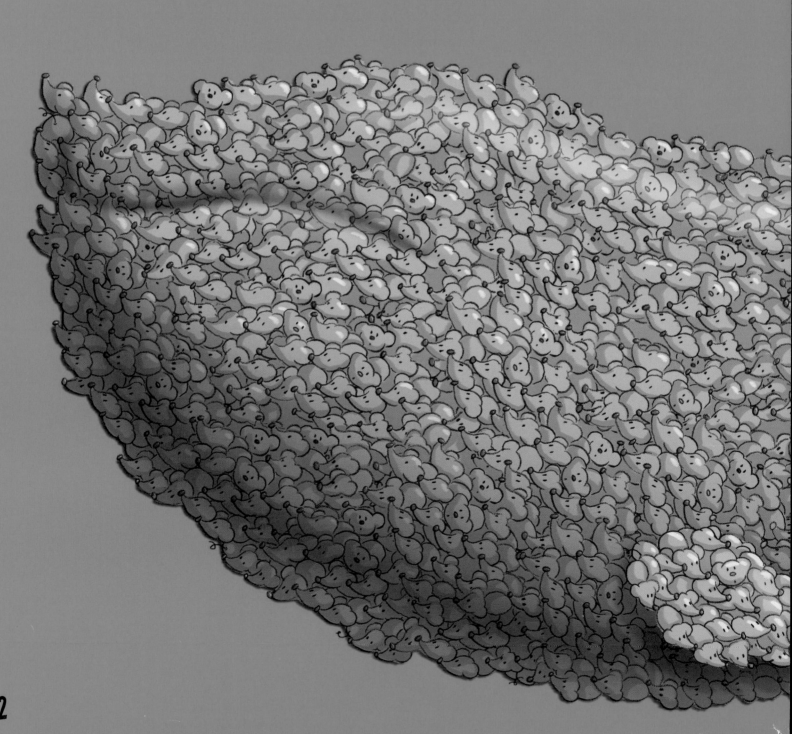

READ MORE

Coffelt, Nancy. *Big, Bigger, Biggest!* New York: Henry Holt and Co., 2009.

Hughes, Susan. *Is It Heavy or Light? What's the Matter?* New York: Crabtree Pub. Company, 2012.

Olson, Nathan. *Heavy and Light: An Animal Opposites Book.* Animal Opposites. Mankato, Minn.: Capstone Press, 2008.

Parker, Vic. *How Heavy Is Heavy?: Comparing Vehicles.* Measuring and Comparing. Chicago: Heinemann Library, 2011.

INTERNET SITES

FactHound offers a safe, fun way to find Internet sites related to this book. All of the sites on FactHound have been researched by our staff.

Here's all you do:

Visit *www.facthound.com*

Type in this code: 9781404883222

Super-cool stuff! Check out projects, games and lots more at **www.capstonekids.com**

Special thanks to our adviser, Terry Flaherty, PhD, Professor of English, Minnesota State University, Mankato, for his expertise.

Editor: Jill Kalz
Designer: Ashlee Suker
Art Director: Nathan Gassman
Production Specialist: Eric Manske
The illustrations in this book were created digitally.

Picture Window Books are published by Capstone,
1710 Roe Crest Drive, North Mankato, Minnesota 56003
www.capstonepub.com

Library of Congress Cataloging-in-Publication Data
Weakland, Mark.
 How heavy? : wacky ways to compare weight / by Mark Weakland; illustrated by Bill Bolton.
  pages cm. — (Wacky comparisons)
 Summary: "Compares various heavy objects to lighter objects in unique, illustrated ways"—Provided by publisher.
 Audience: K to grade 3.
 Includes bibliographical references.
 ISBN 978-1-4048-8322-2 (library binding)
 ISBN 978-1-4795-1912-5 (paperback)
 ISBN 978-1-4795-1908-8 (eBook PDF)
1. Weight (Physics)—Measurement—Juvenile literature. 2. Weight judgment—Juvenile literature. 3. Comparison (Philosophy)—Juvenile literature. I. Bolton, Bill, 1968– illustrator. II. Title.

QC106.W43 2014
530.8—dc23   2013012152

Photo Credit
Capstone/Karon Dubke, 7 (gummy bears)

Printed in the United States of America in North Mankato, Minnesota.
032013   007223CGF13

LOOK FOR ALL THE BOOKS IN THE SERIES:

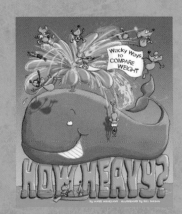

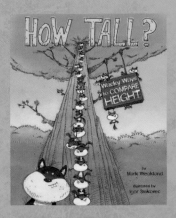